It Won't Work!

By Janine Amos   Illustrated by Annabel Spenceley
Consultant Rachael Underwood

Gareth Stevens Publishing
A WORLD ALMANAC EDUCATION GROUP COMPANY

Please visit our web site at: www.garethstevens.com
For a free color catalog describing Gareth Stevens Publishing's
list of high-quality books and multimedia programs, call
1-800-542-2595 (USA) or 1-800-387-3178 (Canada).
Gareth Stevens Publishing's fax: (414) 332-3567.

Library of Congress Cataloging-in-Publication Data

Amos, Janine.
    It won't work! / by Janine Amos; illustrated by Annabel Spenceley.
        p. cm. — (Courteous kids)
    Includes bibliographical references.
    Summary: Two brief stories demonstrate the importance of staying calm and thinking
about how to solve the problem when things do not work on the first try.
    ISBN 0-8368-3608-1 (lib. bdg.)
    1. Social interaction in children—Juvenile literature.   2. Problem solving in children—
Juvenile literature.   [1. Problem solving.   2. Persistence.   3. Behavior.   4. Conduct of life.]
I. Spenceley, Annabel, ill.   II. Title.
BF723.S62A469   2003
177'.1—dc21
                                                            2002036477

This edition first published in 2003 by
Gareth Stevens Publishing
A World Almanac Education Group Company
330 West Olive Street, Suite 100
Milwaukee, Wisconsin 53212 USA

Series editor: Dorothy L. Gibbs
Graphic designer: Katherine A. Goedheer
Cover design: Joel Bucaro

This edition © 2003 by Gareth Stevens, Inc. First published by Cherrytree Press,
a subsidiary of Evans Brothers Limited. © 1999 by Cherrytree (a member of the
Evans Group of Publishers), 2A Portman Mansions, Chiltern Street, London
W1U 6NR, United Kingdom. This U.S. edition published under license from
Evans Brothers Limited. Additional end matter © 2003 by Gareth Stevens, Inc.

Printed in the United States of America

1 2 3 4 5 6 7 8 9 07 06 05 04 03

Note to Parents and Teachers

The questions that appear in **boldface** type can be used to initiate
discussion with your children or class. Encourage them to think of
possible answers before continuing with the story.

The Sand Castle

Jacob is at the beach with his grandpa.
He is going to build a sand castle.

Jacob fills his pail with sand
and pats the sand down hard.

When Jacob turns the pail over,
the sand falls out.

"It won't work!" Jacob squeals.

Jacob stomps his feet and bursts into tears.

His grandpa hears him.
"You sound very angry, Jacob," says Grandpa.

Jacob cries even harder.

"I can't do it!" he sobs.
How do you think Jacob feels?

"You're having a hard time building a castle
with this sand, aren't you?" Grandpa asks.

12

"Yes," says Jacob, "it keeps falling out of the pail."

13

"What are you going to do?" asks Grandpa.
What do you think Jacob could do?

Jacob looks at the sand. Then he looks at the ocean.
"I'll make the sand wetter!" says Jacob.

15

Jacob mixes water into the dry sand.

He wonders if it will work now.

"I did it!" says Jacob. "It works!"
How do you think Jacob feels now?

18

The Marble Game

Alice is playing with her marble game.
She is putting the pieces of the game together.

She has finished the last tower.
Now she is ready to roll down a marble.

21

Plop! The marble drops straight
to the bottom of the tower.

How do you think Alice feels?

It won't work, thinks Alice.
She looks closely at the game.

What do you think Alice could do?

Alice checks each part of the game.

"Yes!" says Alice. "Here's the problem!"

Alice sees that she put the game together the wrong way. She fixes one of the pieces.

Then she tests the game again.

This time, the marble rolls backward
and forward down the run.

How do you think Alice feels now?

Sometimes things don't work the way we want them to, and we feel frustrated or even angry. When something's not working for you, take a deep breath and tell yourself you can do it. Look at the problem again and try to solve it. If you are very upset, talk to someone about it.

More Books to Read

I Can Do It! Kids Talk About Courage.
Nancy Loewen (Picture Window Books)

I'm Frustrated. Elizabeth Crary (Parenting Press)

Success. Susan Riley (Child's World)